FIND ME IN THE FERAL POCKETS
POEMS FROM THE GOWANUS INTERREGNUM

- EUPHROSINE PUBLISHING -

A portion of proceeds from the initial sale of each copy of this book benefits the Gowanus Dredgers Canoe Club and another portion benefits the Lenape Center.

BOOK I
OF THE

JöKULHLAUP

FIND ME IN THE FERAL POCKETS

POEMS FROM THE GOWANUS INTERREGNUM

BRAD VOGEL

ALSO BY BRAD VOGEL

Broad Meadow Bird: 15 Years of Poetry

ALSO BY EUPHROSINE PUBLISHING

Yellowbird: A True Tale of the Early Settlement of Town Schleswig

———————————

Cover (*Green Heron and Gowanus Canal coal tar rainbows near the 9th Street Bridge*)
Back Cover (*Image of floating dead rat - a "Gowanus football"*)
Cover, back cover & interior artwork, all by the author

Cover & Book Design: Nicole Vergalla www.nvergalla.com
Author photo by Nicole Vergalla

A note on the cover font: created by Nicole Vergalla from the letters hand-carved into an Egyptian Revival tomb in Green-Wood Cemetery where she often birds with the author in the early morning, the font is called Anna Delafield after one of the prominent names inscribed upon the vault (restored not long before initial publication of this book).

Epigraphs:

Journal of Jasper Danckaerts, *Visiting Gouanes*, 1679
Library of Congress, *American Notes: Travels in America*, 1750 to 1920 Collection

The Gas Drip Bard, on Gowanus, 1898
The Brooklyn Daily Eagle

Julian T. Brolaski, *gowanus atropolis*, 2011
Ugly Duckling Presse, included with permission of the author

Elizabeth Henaff, *Invisible Inhabitants*, 2017
NYU Journal of Design and Science, included with permission of the author

ISBN: 979-8-218-37344-3
Printed in United States of America
First Edition

No AI was used, at least not intentionally, in the creation of this work.

"An ancient and despoiled waterway provides Brad Vogel with a vehicle for conveying New York, history, the whole starry swirl overhead. So much glints in this collection: subway flash, distant skyscrapers, the smeared walls of dumptrucks. It echoes Whitman, who termed the same landscape "liquid, sane, unruly, musical, self-sufficient." Both poets reminding us that the mystery of New York is in the water."

- RUSSELL SHORTO, AUTHOR OF *THE ISLAND AT THE CENTER OF THE WORLD*

"Every superfund site deserves clear-eyed, contrarian, steadfast love poems like Brad Vogel's to Gowanus Canal. He sees it all from his canoe and names it all--black mayonnaise, xylened waters, light through the milkweed--and loves Gowanus anyway."

- KATHLEEN FLENNIKEN, AUTHOR OF THE POETRY COLLECTION *PLUME*

"Vogel displays a persistent haiku sensibility in these poems, which in turn displays a depressive mind turning to (and freshening) lyricism to alleviate its own suffering. As in his own canoe-wandering in Gowanus, this chapbook offers a journey through a strange, miraculous and charming poetic mind."

- TAWANDA MULALU, AUTHOR OF *PLEASE MAKE ME PRETTY,*
I DON'T WANT TO DIE: POEMS

"Brad Vogel's Find Me In The Feral Pockets conjures vivid images of Brooklyn's Gowanus Canal and its environs, revealing the wild ecology hidden amidst the urban wasteland—but it soon becomes an apt metaphor to explore human self-reflection and direction. In exhuming forgotten local histories to be intertwined with intimate verse, Vogel explores love, loathing, and survival in the big city via a sense of longing for and belonging to a singular place."

- JOSEPH ALEXIOU, AUTHOR OF *GOWANUS: BROOKLYN'S CURIOUS CANAL*

"Brad Vogel's passion for the Gowanus - as local history, as ecological niche, as metaphor, as a tiny bit of feral life still left in NYC - shines through every poem in this wonderful collection."

- HUGH RYAN, AUTHOR OF *WHEN BROOKLYN WAS QUEER*

"Steeped in the murky, mysterious waters of the Gowanus Canal, these poems invite us along on nocturnal adventures and solitary voyages, revealing unexpected beauty and camaraderie amidst a precarious landscape. Vogel immerses us into a community in flux, digging up buried toxins and bringing night dwellers into the light."

- NATHAN KENSINGER, JOURNALIST & FILMMAKER OF *BLACK MAYONNAISE*

"Got the chills reading this. The words and cadences transported me right back to an early morning paddle on the Gowanus."

- MICHELLE YOUNG, FOUNDER UNTAPPED CITIES,
AUTHOR *SECRET BROOKLYN: AN UNUSUAL GUIDE*

"Find Me In The Feral Pockets is a vivid and beautiful collection about emotion, truth and the dark environments of the Gowanus Canal, its history rippling through the verse. These waters have rarely inspired anything so tender and observational. Perhaps you'll look at them differently now after reading."

- GREG YOUNG OF THE BOWERY BOYS PODCAST

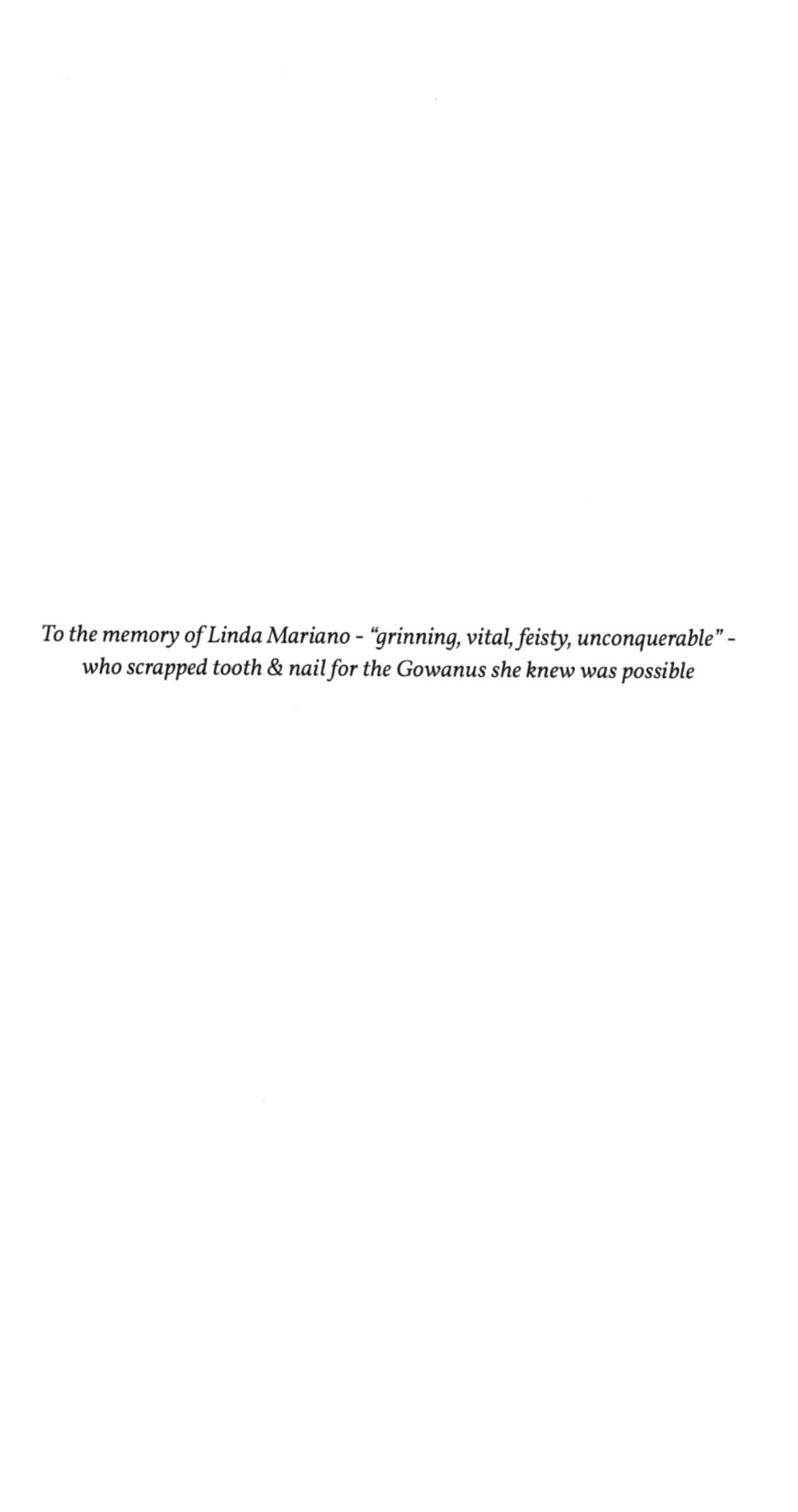

*To the memory of Linda Mariano - "grinning, vital, feisty, unconquerable" -
who scrapped tooth & nail for the Gowanus she knew was possible*

"We let it penetrate us thoroughly."
JOURNAL OF JASPER DANCKAERTS, VISITING GOUANES, 1679

"The smells, Oh! so horrid, would almost set you crazy /
But I'm told in that neighborhood the people seldom die."
THE GAS DRIP BARD, ON GOWANUS, 1898

"one draws forth from the banks"
JULIAN T. BROLASKI, *GOWANUS ATROPOLIS*, 2011

"Under the hypothesis that anything living there must possess mechanisms
to counteract the toxic cocktail it steeps in, we set out to document this
environment slated for destruction"
ELIZABETH HENAFF, *INVISIBLE INHABITANTS*, 2017

Highly subjective, scale-less, all at once - Gowanus across the Interregnum, 2016-2024

A Map o' the Creek, Millponds, Basins, Street Ends, Bulkheads, & Feral Pockets

UPON REALIZING YET AGAIN I AM NOT TRAPPED IN THE STEEL JAWS OF DEATH
for Jee Leong Koh

They wanted me to be
Confessional
But this was the best I could do
With Gowanus
Dino maws menacing
Even at rest
Pigeons and ripples
Steel ruins and trucks
As the sun slithers
Sweetgum by sweetgum
Toward my secrets
Shell fragments, deforms
Inside
Notion of non-penetration
Always going deepest
When it finally hits
And organs get
Involved
Forcing me to cry out

I am a coward
I am a lunatic
I am a sappy hopeless foolhardy delusional romantic
I am caustic with unwarranted anger
I am trixy when I'm weak
I am far, far, far too old
I suspect I am broken for good
I worry I want to be taken care of

What was I thinking?
Of course the cactus
Will get what it wants
In the bereftness
Dog park desert

I could not cross
Littered with saurian skulls

I throw my canteen high
Fire wild at the parking lot sky
Say good-bye
Last water scatters

Do not tell me it
Will get better
Just sit silent
And look
Watch the scars try
To callous
The tree try
To leaf
In dry high winds

Tyrannical
Jaw still clenched off
Across the canal
Droplets flowing now
Superfund and Expressway
And I am here now
My shadow pops up
To tell me
A dark patch
On the gravel
Pulsing at periphery
Breath barely registering

Butts and bottle caps
Bollards and weeds
Scraps and sun

Profile sharpens
Pile of wants and thoughts
Silhouette of busted needs

BLACK MAYONNAISE
for Katia Kelly

Sick rainbows swirl
Deep secrets bubble up
Past percolating at low tide
- And here I stand
Bulkheaded, reeking
Ancient timbers bowed
A sponge garden
With a runoff problem

I envy you, Gowanus
We envy you, Gowanus
You have an EPA
To rid you of your PCBs
A Superfund
For your black mayonnaise

Would that I could
Would that we would
Dredge ours up
Omissions and failings
Dredge ours up
Half lives and toxic words
Mix sludge mountains
With concrete
To stabilize
And cart it all away
To some other state

But up through a
Skimming of sewage
A coal tar crest emerges
Surfaces, splashing

A cormorant thought
Up from impenetrable depths

Wings shiver
In spite of itself
Life persists -
No administrator needed

MOUTHING THE WORDS

Some days poems are lips
to suck all the venom out
- when you thought kiss

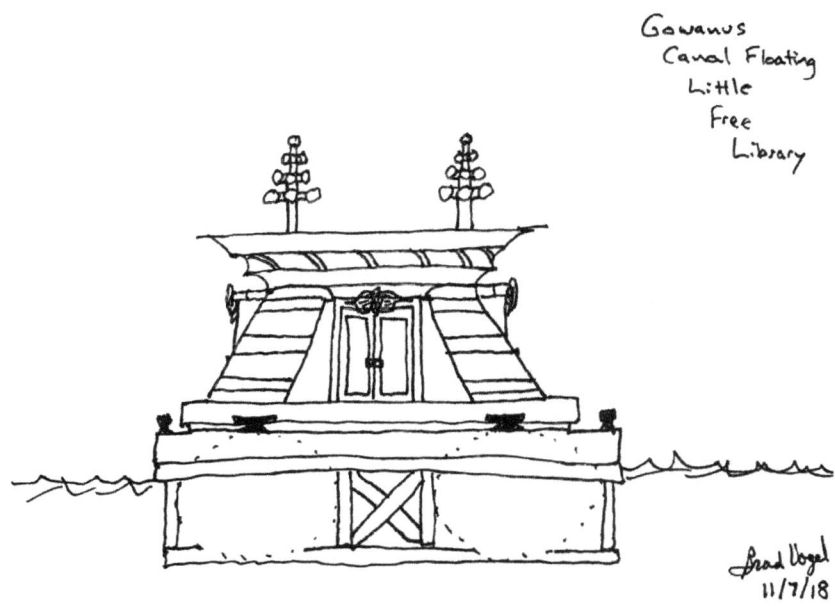

Gowanus
Canal Floating
Little
Free
Library

THE UNPLANNED PLACE
after Nathan Kensinger & Nate Dorr's "Reclaimed Ground"

We must intend the cormorant's every perch
Every path through flora
Must be concerted

We must control each pebble's placement
Every hint of compost must not generate

Only the waves remain
Consistent through all phases
Looking on with ancient eyes
Sighing, as if offering smoke,
Gesturing gently saying
"Chill, man, chill"
Lest we lose the very nature
Of the wild green hill

Maybe the phoenix
Did not spring
orange from fire
But slowly emanated
Green, barely noticeable
Rising from rust
Teased from rustle
Of withered Queens lace
Hovered tentatively its
Blue tails up from debris
Trees of heaven truly
Framing canted remnant piles

In a megalopolis
Our minds thirst for
The unplanned
For the feral pockets
The water remains unbound

But the land is always conquered
Grand parks get us almost there
But then we learn that Olmsted
Envisioned every tree, moved each
And we despair again
For our minds sense mirage
And not the real magic
That rarest spice of today's city
The unplanned place
A space left for nature
And people to
Pick their dance partners
At random
And tango at will
Or breakdance
In reclamation
Of the real, the possible
The dirt, the weeds
The at last again dreamable

TOXIC FOAM PEOPLE
(GOWANUSIANS)

for Peter Reich

We jostle the barrier
Quivering
Parts per million jiggling
Undiluted
We're at our worst
Fragile
Death froth
Sad beauty
Our past mistakes
Churned up
Mixed with clean air

The tide alone
Is not enough
Nor the flushing tunnel

Shimmy and shake
Shiver and quake
Eons-old
Salt water sacs

But I suppose
While you exist
Be as cloud-like as you can
Float serene
Sparkle a bit on closer inspection
Wink before you go
Effervesce

Give that kid
At the street-end
- who wasn't planning to care
A beautiful dream

MUMMICHOGS

Is it sex
Is it the fight for sex
Is it practice in hot shallows
The darting slash flashing
Petro blue
Fletching yellow
Blackened stripes
Stretched catseye marbles
Churning
Practice for escaping
The inevitable
Night heron beaks

Or is this nature
Like a ghost
Trying to speak
Under surface
In torsioned ripples
To us dockside
Paranormal investigators
Of something
Since childhood
Innately known:

I am a weeble wobble
I cannot fall down
Punch me
And I will rock back
Only to lay you low

And all we hear
Through our 700-channel
Electromagnetic amplifier
Through heavy static is

weeb
rock back
low

So we sit and scurrilously
Sift
Through splashes set in sun
For more clues
Call in Merrill
For his Ouija board
To discern
If these are lost
Beck songs
Black sediments
Are giving up

Perhaps these airpods
Cigarettes in my ears
Will tell

No put them away
Set aside your sensors
And hear faint splash choruses
Going in crowds
Listen for the beat of night wings

I think it's sex
And the fight for sex
There in xylened waters
Toileted rocks
Off our sponge park
Though articles say they stay
Defiant mummichogs
In their estuaries

maybe they've gone
   Chemosynthetic
   Like deep sea venters
Who forget
The sun

Which trips at last
Down through
Al Capone's church
And is it sex
The fight for sex
That roils these rainbows
Or practice in lukewarm shallows
For shadows
  Thrusting

The night heron
  Thrusting
His sleek sulfurous crown

IT'S TIME

Whether it exists or not
I will carry it with me
Whether you know it or not
We must take it with us
Like the seawater we
Built our bodies to enclose
A thermos for our explorations
Or instinct with its bundled sticks
Low hooting bassoon
That and self-will as it
Too falls before analysis
And weapons-grade technology
We take that rucksack for the journey
But however we must circumscribe it
Find a tote for a dial
For whatever sun comes into view
Hold the spinning hourglass
Listen to uranium's cackle decrescendo
And count your blessings
When you're far, far
From the homes you know

NOT IN FACT DEAD

after Bonnie Ralston's "Benthic"
at the Gowanus Dredgers Canoe Club Boathouse

Hope but fear
they are broken dreams
not even nightmares
but oxygen-deprived raisins
far from the sun
deferred sure but isn't
the more unnerving
part of their spins
the unearthing
and the presentation
seeing the strings attached
wandering through benthic
can't-even-fester-so-dessicate
stone alien embryos suspended
and I wonder if that one
with the rusty torqued tail
is my age five dream to be a
paleontologist and make pizza
at Rocky Roccoco's in Sheboygan
I think I know them
wandering boathouse labyrinthine
they're more frightening
in wan morning light -
but these dreams are always
different up close
and even then it's not
quite intimate enough
I'm always intrigued to
dive my eyes further
deeper in
hoping I have the fine tuned
bow thruster control
but wary all the same

that I'm zooming in
for microscopy
to keep from seeing
sensing
reeling
from great mucked totality
accumulated cloud pile
of roadkilled daydreams
I did not ask for this
retrospective of my
roads not taken
but here swarms they silent
gyrating hollow whispers
and I know by
how they twirl inanimate
that the Canal's to blame
once again
fetid frenemy
the beaten imp
tricksier surely
with each dredged scoop
so I stand back against
grimy canoe racks
and realize this
is probably the armada
they are waiting for in
some far flung corner
of our universe
so the artist is once again
I think
rightly the savior
how we can sometimes barely
see the seeds we've sown
right there grotesque
defenses girding their hopes
floating right in front of us

CARCINOGENS AND SHIT
AND NEW YORK CITY

Why canoe this cess?
Why does one's soul here beg such
chemotherapy?

A POSTCARD I CANNOT WRITE

for Christopher P. Bernhardt

I wish I had a fireplace
And Louis XIV furniture
So I could hurl it all in
Burn it
Desperately
And you could see my face
Roiling
With blue flames
So I had a way
To tell you
So you could know
How things have been

OUT IN THE STYX

Flashing like silver
As a musket
To a Marylander
 I grip tight
 My paddle
  Bright
      And
      Keen

Creosote breaths
A skein with a sheen
Chest heaves
As I lean
Out
In
Out
In
The sticks
Hit the rim
Beat the drum
In and out
Out and in

Out in the Styx
Just me and him solo
Surfacing merganser
Wide-eyed paddler
Dawn whispers in periwinkle
Droplets drip the blade
How free are we
Am I
Here BQE-framed
Lavender-lapped
Far from
Cerberus'd shore

Out in the Styx
Is that char on that shotgun
Or is it this heat?
Or an egret
Lighting out
Over flood-buckled streets
Past Pitot grapefruits
Looping locquats
Through wet blossoms
To the sheets
How I miss you
How you made me
Take the bayou
Take the streets

Out in the Styx
Reeds riot green
And so do I
Who do you know best
And how do you know him?
- There is no better way
      to get to know a person
      than in canoe
      under sky
Under willows
Under gnats
Under storm petrel hover hum
Permission to speak freely
It starts to come
At ease, at ease
Bendering
Meanding
Out in my element
Though not out:
There lie
Depths below
Undeniably tamarack black

We adjust
- always avoiding the tip

Out in the Styx
Ghost crowds
Watch from bulwarks
As bittern booms
Lumberwinging by
Trailing translucent past
Fuzz fire at fin
Jared Kushner
And our sins
Bury bodies
Across from Whole Foods
Plate-sized
Oysters
Spill out onto
Tugboats
Crushing my bow now
Canal, millpond, creek
Coal tar gasified leak
In
Out
Past and Present
Duck and sneak
Like my words
Through Darby's Patch
And glassy peaks
On tides and
Flushing tunnels
Their scent corrosive orange
A merganser's beak
Sharp as truth
That we seek
Like a girl
Throwing petals
On putridity

Rectractile dreamer
Tracks the streak
Swirled from my paddle
In this uncertainty
In this din
In and out
Out and in
In the Styx
In the Styx
Out in the Styx

QUEUE - 3.17.18

And will this flash before my eyes as I die
Dog barking here in Rite Aid
As I force my chip card in
Hope to god it sticks
Physically bracing
Hey Joe rumbling in one earbud
The girl bagging
Tho you said no bag
Peripherally he unloads
Minding bulk baby carriage
Morning sun sears it all
Can I hear the slight hiss
Or is that the plastic bag being revoked
Or this feeling
Like some joker's in there
Chain smoking menthols
In my veins
This moment fizzing
Coursing evanescent as it's pan—fried
Salted hard
Pissed up like skata
And set aside
For hospital bed tube jungle
Or fire metal scream on a bridge at night
However I go

The slide will be ready
But will the projector pick
Click
Lock this one into place
As the kinetoscope
Fire whirs slice scenes one last time

Will my fingers feel as cold
Will I see you
Or us
Or will I feel slight tug of alpaca sweater
As she hands me the receipt

QUESTIONS FOR
GOWANUS WHITEFISH
for Gary Francis

Well hello there, Gowanus whitefish
What stories do you tell tonight
What floating tales of interactivity?

Did you come from a penthouse lair?
From a public housing project stair?
From a place of hope, a place of despair?

From whence were you flushed
You and your neutrally-buoyant brethren?

A school of magnums
Tickles our paddles
Heading harborward

Were you the evidence?
Were you broke?
Were you fulfilled?

Unifiers, speak
Burble up
Naphthalene helixes

Uniters
Used
Undoubtedly
Fucking
Our waterways

THE TRAIN SAYS LOVE

The train says love
And I
Don't say no
But I tangle myself
Trying
Through cold-dewed leaves
To say anything else

The train says love
And ticker tapes
Toward Manhattan
So close now
I'm left yearning
In all directions
Trestle clouds and click and clack

The train says love
But says it slant
Flies the flag
Rides a sun-bottomed viaduct
Over this problem
This soot streaked confoundity
This volcano under Gowanus
This, here leaning,
On iron stairs

HOW TO SURVIVE THE CITY

Bubble-like
I leap lightly
Across whirring
Half-formed tufts
Radiating from a
Gargantuan city sagebrush
From pinnacle to pinnacle
Great skyscraper pincushion
Grinding on
And I dance
Barely touched by the
Sandstorm shitshow
A chamois
Bounding for his life
But be-smiled
Unbesmirched
Toes launching from
Lightning rods
Rotating unrelentingly
Wild with a hopeless hope
Set crackling
Through it all

WRITEN WHILE STANDING JUST NOW PARTIALLY DRUNK ON CARROLL STREET

Who knew
olive drab shorts
could hide that much
or not hide,
really
broadcast
tantalize
insanify
rile up waterspouts
of twice-distilled
thirst
and yet not that alone
but spread
a sort of live
more green
unnameable blanket
safe,
like I said,
truly
an undeniable weight
remind me fully
that the dream is not just a dream
that tea and crumpets
did, in fact
ride the slide
down my gullet
hit me in a place
i did not know
sits inside
make the olive drab veil
a beacon of welcome
a ticket to ride

MODE FOR MAKING DUE

i step off the plank
depart dock in dark

and i know why i clambered
aboard this shadow ship
in particular
for a quick zip
how its name is my condition

how the good boat battleshort
came along when my fuses
felt most ready to blow
and gowanus bay loomed

how she took me
she and her feathered femme fatale
her mustaschioed charon
out to a condition

military equipment gets placed in
so it can't shut down
when circumstances
would otherwise
damage the equipment
the personnel

here my brain and body
battleshorted
breathe in bunker fuel
and bunker fins
bliss of barely seeing
black rubber
harbor breeze

this mode of sovereignty
emerges only here
where water
wombs me
fends and bumpers
the land's bullshitocracy
of faux fugues and pains
the piled unknowable losses

water
water dissolves the
gordian knots

we say them see them be them again
"I think we did the right thing."

and i
lay down my sword
on the bunker launch
on the other side
step ashore
from ferry
fuses still somehow
functional
smoking a bit
glowing
cauterized
possibly even partially healed
in the wide, once-barking
now admonished
night

LIGHT THROUGH THE MILKWEED

for Nora Almeida and Martin Bisi

Light through the milkweed
Sun through the leaves
Canal set to quilting
In the slightest of breeze
Inches from ripples
A cormorant stealths home
Winds down to his harbor
And I'm left alone
May 21 2020 7-7:45 am
What will the sun see
If it takes me for dock
As my veins go translucent
Legs crossed on this rock
Starlings quark on locust
I hate that I know season
For summer's always winter tinged
When man gets hold of reason
Loader bulls, reflects in quaver
Seaside golden rod aquiver
I melt with frap like a Dali clock
The concrete plant and I a river
Honest Gowanus anomalousness
Juneberries and cloud of sparrows
Work your morning acupuncture
Nebulize me with your arrows
For bindweed twines and boas me
Hours dervish, ache madly round
A mind suspended, harried, worn
By an idling engine and cheeping sounds
They told me to stay at home
To pause

And so I am here
Water whipped
Wing warped
No matter what time it is
No matter what time is
No matter, time
No time

THE LATE MR. AND MR. ESTUARIAL

Four years
Athwart silent canoe
Years become tides
In and out
Ripple blur eyes
My memories of you
Flow
Eddy
Empress tree branches
Slip twilight gowns
Slip mummied husks
Whole trees die
Others grow in place
Full flow fails
Reverses
Accelerates
Resumes
Rises

Afloat
In stinking rot
In perfect sunrise
I remember us at our best
I remember me at my worst

Clamped geese
Watch me nervous nest-top
I do not blame them
I remember me at my best
I remember us at our worst

Was it betrayal
Impure and simple
- or great
Hissing mother goose in me
Exploding ONKK
Protecting the truth of eggs
My own future selves
Lying potent bankside?

Tides warp
Seeds rounden
Yolks harden
Peck from inside

Half-dead roach
Surfs slow brown gyres
On a shit-slime board
Seaward
In the end

All I can do
Is voyage on
Light on my lifejacket
Paddle hacking softly
Endlessly
At that old knot
Of contrariety

Bow set for home

I WONDER IF THE JULIUS' HAMBURGER

could possibly be enough
be dinner
be meal
with me now
no I will not
have a Coke with you
that is not at all
realistic
nay, this life now
rings more bereft
I dig the Beatles
F train home
comforted drunk
lonely as fuck
odd ass duck
swimming round
circling
who knows what
mind searing circuit
board smoking truths
I swirl round the bend
all the signs say
end
canal wends
black black dark
done
no fun no sun
I see myself in skyscrapers
nonchalant but
built privileged
popped into existence not
by me
DNA here spinning
out useless I guess
wondering if I
need to be more

radical to justify
brief buffeted ballast blowing
existence
a boy
who dreamed empires
now wary of them
apparently
you can imitate anyone you want
because
I dig
old Tony
Bennett
but ain't it
no longer
than anything
you see
       -         what am I motherfucking
dancing round
all these words
thoughts
non javelins fired
without thinking
those are the points
scaffolding and cones
graffiti, stickers, tomatoes
bamboo, black helmet
I blink my hands
Jeeps honks, blazes forth
I walk across
stand in light
wibbling a bit inside
just admit you're depressed
let the cargo spill
say it
burn your thousand excuses
rise up true
in the mirror
in a nest of ashes

A CARROLL STREET HAUNT
for Ute Zimmerman

When rambling soused down Nevins
Be sure to rub your eyes and look
At code emblazoned across the night
Blaring "ALEX IGL A LLC"

Perhaps it's just the pale ale talking
Or some scrap of a long lost book
But no one's sure of these blood red words
Yowling "ALEX IGL A LLC"

I thought it a mirage of miasma
Hovering from canal's rank crook
Sneering, skipping blue rivets toward me
Chanting "ALEX IGL A LLC"

Street stones swirled beneath me
I squinted hard, my body shook
Only a Strong Rope could save me now from
Hissing "ALEX IGL A LLC"

Letters dwarfed the food trucks now
Harsh letters strangely took
Puffed form of a great night frigatebird
Croaking "ALEX IGL A LLC"

Pressed by this crimson throat sac
Sweating, reeling, so forsook
I stumbled as the street lights flickered
Wailing "ALEX IGL A LLC"

Scarlet, scarlet – all I could see
So close my mind began to cook
And I ran, all fevered, for putrid waters
Cackling back "ALEX IGL A LLC"

Pounding planks I jumped the rail
I flailed in darkness for some hook
And the red glow named me as I hit these waters I still haunt
As "ALEX IGL A LLC"

PLEASE FORGIVE ME,
FUTURE MAYBES
for Katie Bishop

I want you to see
great-grandchildren of my
niece floating a century
off how the folly felt -
port-a-john trucks
asphalt trucks
arizona ice tea trucks
pipe trucks
dump trucks
cement trucks
moving trucks
street sweepers
and oh so
innocent buses
how they all stood
here on a bright leafed
Gowanus morning
killing me with subtlest blades
pushing you into artificiality
or possible non-existence
how mundane the particulate matters
how birds celebrated
devoid of alarm
how men walked in hoodies
and washed sidewalks
how I sipped my bottle
of frappuccino on the stoop
as teams across the street
started up oil trucks
and I surveyed a stream
of bicyclists
encased in rumblings

wondered if they
-      you?   -
stood a chance
how, I thought
did I get my bottle
my paper
this pen

CONCRETE THOUGHTS

Fiery triceratops skulls know winter is coming
By bulky bureaucratic beige-tastic blandity

Rope-bridged between these
    I sway
Asphalt planks
Cables twined of mugwort
Seaside goldenrod
      Parole officers pa
          troll below

Permanently bathed in red light
I don't need sign blare emphatic
To tell me
Through growl-whir chants
Of each turnaround car
Stalked by black and white orbs of the state
    This is the END

Here on 2nd
Between 5th and 4th
Though there is no 4th
Only a Basin to guide me
And it took just a second or three
Amidst dogbane bothered bottles
To figure out if this was all a ruse

This feral pocket where our CSOs
Avalanche when gods weep uncontrollably
Human waste heading for herons
And hoping for the filtrations
Of ribbed mussels

This rife patch where old Belgian block
Collapses, Knieveling out over the brink

Facing down a hangry Gowanus
And slowly losing the encounter
Bulkheads still blowing out
As if the made land's
Belt could not handle
All these meals of carcinogens
With time for dessert

Here, rope-bridged, I sit
Slung, musing
Caught between creek-side tulip tree
Mùxulhemënshi
Giver of Lenape canoes
And concrete blocks
The Sleeper's toys
Where I first joined the Dredgers
In exile, as Gary paddle-boarded by
Red, toxic-bottomed canoes
Locked by a box that advised
CHILLAX

On a rope bridge anchored
By a sinking, musket-sparing
Marylander hand
Disappearing into muck
Redcoat shot pelting the calamus
As Washington weeps on the hill
And a billionaire mother trying to escape
Through great hollow flooding garages
Come down from the 35th floor
Her children wailing
In thrice-rezoned future
As hurricane surge breaches
The great mouth gate
One final time

- Here I muse at the cast

Sewer cover constellations
And know at last
What the sign means

I lay rope-bridged
Looking for the few stars
And La Guardia-bound
Meteors through
Gas-drip willow leaves
In a trick garden
Native but not native
Chemicals creeping up
With full aroma
Here between my
Ankle-bracelet fitting
And the incessant beeping
Of my 1st or 3rd
Midnight salt pickup
Between the dredger
Lifejacketed on his barge
And the secretary
Whose shawl remains
In fluorescent rain
Black through the windows
High overhead
Here between full-leafed
Trees of heaven and
Their dying branches
Between chained S.S. Oops
And sad coffee break benches
Between sleeping buses
Tourist red and Orthodox yellow
And a glacial outwash plain
Between tugboats bulling
Between belabored barges
And a kid on his bike
With a camera

And nothing better to do
Egret-rouser
Gosling-noticer
Laugher-at-fences
Hearer-of-ever-rushing-waters-somewhere-deep-below
Absorber-of-cyan-glow-of-great-towering-future-tide-clock
Between heavy June twilight
And the hard all-sumac rise
Of a February dawn

All these rope bridges
I cross at once, at risk
Intersect in me
Radiate out from me
Undulates of some strange, time-spanning
Extremophile tide
Rays working out slowly
From some dark Gowanus sun

I hold these rusted green railings
And walk across
In all directions

BRIDGE BETWEEN BRIDGES
for Nene Humphrey

I am on a bridge
  And you are on a bridge
  And we are on a bridge
     In gray mist in the morning

A bridge between bridges
  From green arced to blue
  A span between silhouettes
     - standing me, standing you

I've never met you
  You've never met me
    Except this cloud catwalk
       Has brought us to be

Here, suspended in fog
  On a bridge between bridges
  A smile formed in silence
     Slung from a hint of sun

EXTREMOPHILES

Deep in muck, just our luck
Science heralds extremophiles
-        But then we'd always known
Always been
Our superfund kinship
Buried in our guts
Methane eaters
Wizened heat seekers
Archaea rooting
Down epochs
Toward new selves
Though beset by hostility

> Bring me a tugboat they say
> Kick up the sick sed, make my day
> Let me eat, let me morph, let me play
> Down, far from Gowanus blues
> At dark bottoms of bowed basins

Who that canoes
Berated from the bridges
Is not
In their guts
An extremophile?

> For it's a more visceral love
> One from the tract
> Not the heart
> One that's no act
> But an art
> Chorused we Canal's extremophiles

Look at them eat, look at them go
All unicellular from head to toe
What will they do

When the bucket comes
To take their feast of poison
This strange bathymetric buffet
The leavings of our failings
Are their ripe hours d' oeuvres today
Plenty of mayo for their sandwiches
Down past sharp ribbed mussels
Wedged in silent sturdy stations
Who cling and make their way

> Shall I make a form?
> Shall I give a name?
> Whoo will run the tests?
> Whooo will play the game
> In the stench of the old creek's ghost?

Hardy little buggers these
Under waves plutonic bent
Evolving for strange tasks at hand
Tools organic somehow sent

> What of these waters
> When we're gone
> What of our piles
> Of man's decay
> Who will eat the sewage
> On a grim, cold, shit gray day?

Who are we to look down our noses
We with the noses
We lovers of extremes
At extremophiles
What's wrong with new combos
Said the DNA?
What will they find on the slide
Under the scope
Behind your membrane?

Have our paddles stirred
Thine rancid elderberry wine
To your liking
Wild one?
What is it like to be buried
Why do you shit where you eat
These are the questions that ebullate
To aficios of toxins and pressure and heat

> We are the ones
> You've been praying for
> The tall jungle stand
> Rife with keys
> But you slash us too to forget
> All your potions to battle disease
> Cleanup is only cleanup
> In a certain feeble
> Scarecrow sense

A killdeer shriek-whines a-wing
Past steel pilings to brick yard gravel
Kicking up thrill as eyes and head follow
-       What is he trying to protect?
What treasure lies a ways under waves
Downstream, the decidedly other way

What bes thee, trove
For which I and others strove
What gnostic knowledge hides
Popping out now and then
To sun like a mud crab
From a bulkhead crevice
What do we need from you
What feral antidote do you
Proffer in your slimes
Your tunicate turnicate sunbursts
Galaxies exploding silently

B. VOGEL

Under every sludgy
Rock

I put on my rockweed floaties
Wreathe the wrack about wrists
Make myself a monster child
Doggy paddle out, no Swain suit
Into the black lagoon
How could one so many ages old
Be - and want to be -
So unbrackish, so unsloughed
So willfully, bladder-bouyed
Naive

Here off Cape Creosote
Where factory once pumped shine
By benthic bulge at *Beautiful Blue*
I swirl in Iris' brine
I double check the settings on myself
On my remotely operated underwater drone
And I head down into them
Jauntily toward Gowanus' waters
I go

I feel an eel, buffleheads skitter in my wake
Through old channels crooked on an Eymund map
Through whipped undulations of Gary's fly line
I dive, I burrow, I bury, I snake
Into the petrochemical state of my kind
Into the sedimental bind of my mind
Down into Gowanus
To see what I find

Movement in dark
What is your extremity
A thing you are
Or a thing you've made
Do you love it
Because you must
Or because you cannot not
-        Or because
By being you
Know the greater thing
Is cloven

Floating Shrine for the Return of the Menhaden, Gowanus Bay (2020)

MORNING IN GOWANUS

I see the sea's heartbeat
here in Gowanus
wonder if it's mine

as I too
am doing better
less frantic
in our undulations
flowing more
for living
mornings
now beginnings

I touch my wrist
hear whisper roarings
from inside distant
conch shell capillaries
shush shush
    -            the pulse is good

the pulse is flood
basin fills ventricular
the sun rises
through Dyke's Lumber
mural-grown
saltgrass

chambers fill
make me me
full current

what a sloshing
in one-ish
place and time
waves of photons
waves of gravity
waves of carbon
waves of sea

what a conclave

what a we

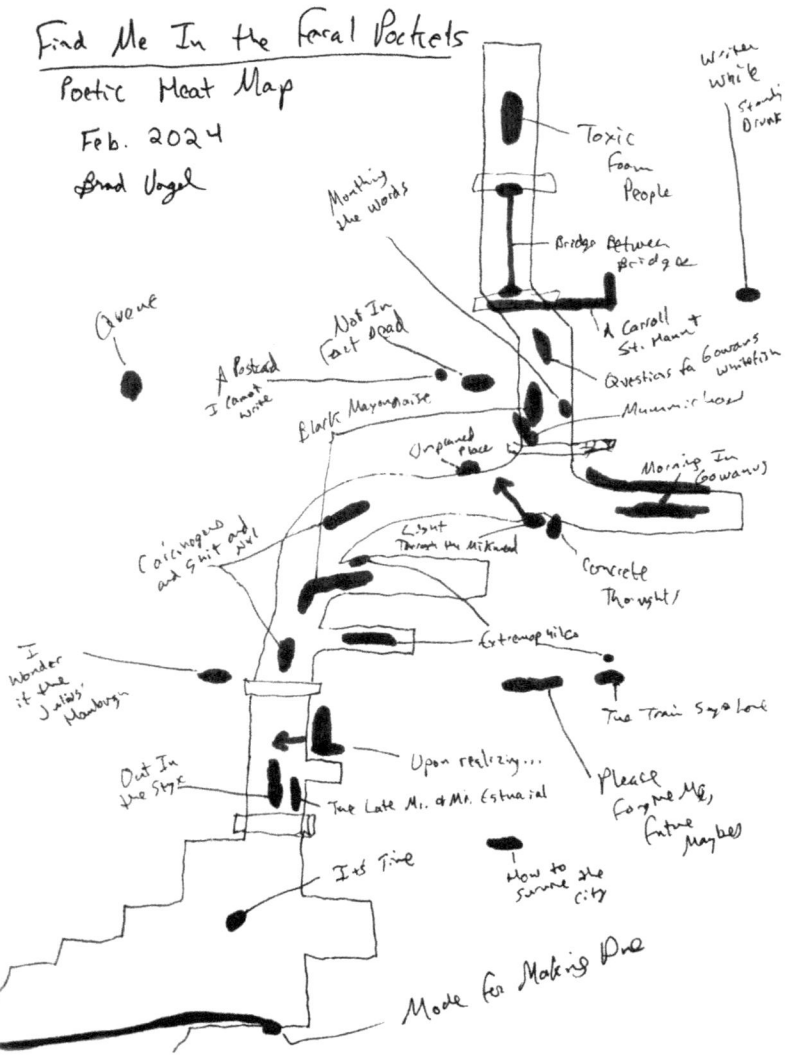

Credits:

The poem "Postcard I Cannot Write" first appeared in *Smartish Pace*, where it was a finalist for the Erskine J. Poetry Prize.

The poem "It's Time" first appeared in the *Fresh Water Review*.

The poem "Concrete Thoughts" first appeared at *Deadline Gowanus*.

Thanks To:

For making it happen: Jee Leong Koh, Levan Iordanashvili, Nicole Vergalla, Melissa Nilles, JEM, Yousuf and Sadia Siddiqui, Paul Onyx Lozito and Benedict Campbell, Rob Phansalkar, David Groff, Christopher Encarnacion, Rob Rossmeissl

For providing a platform: Karin Coonrod, Katie Bishop, Marin Gazzinaga, Jerry Wagoner, Bonnie Ralston, Jason Sahler, Katarina Jerinec, Melody Bates, Kristine Esser Slentz, Danielle Butler, Karen Karbiener, Capt. Jonathan Boulware, Zak Risinger, Jennifer Juneau, David Sharps, Molly Garfinkel, Carolina Salguero, Stephen Reichert, N.D. Austin, Benjamin Shepherd, Kristine Esser Slentz, Nate Dorr, Poets Settlement

For opening the Gowanus gates: Owen Foote, Gary Francis, Nicole Vergalla, Celeste LeCompte, Jos Prol, Liz Rabson Schnore, Eymund Diegel, Ashley Privett, Sasha Chavchavedze, Miska Draskoczy, Chris Reynolds and Jamie Courville, Matthew Cline, Ute Zimmerman, Bart Chezar, Nene Humphrey, Jessica Dalrymple, Rita Ormsby, Corinne Brenner, Peter Reich, Martin Bisi, Vienna Carroll, Jack Riccobono, Miranda Sielaff, Marie Viljoen, Pam Wong, Kelsey Butterworth, Andrew Lenaghan, Jenna Scherer, Rob Hon, Stefan Dreisbach-Williams, Lillian Ruiz, Karen Blondel, Harvey Rehal, Kelly Sanford, Kate Murray, Nora Almeida, Katia Kelly, Marlene Donnelly, Steve M., Garrett Benisch, MODUS, Sandye Renz, Rich Garr, Uriah + Anna, Iviva Olenick, Ed Woodham, the Gowanus dawn readers

Special thanks to: Capt. Mary Habstritt, Gryg Tarianik, Joan K. Davidson, Patrick Nason and Elisha Omar, my family, Karl Elder, Gabriel Gudding, Barbaralee Diamonstein-Spielvogel, Gia Anansi-Shakur, Olesya Bondar, the Principles denizenry and staff, Piero Iberti, Jason Koo, Amanda Hollander, Chris Shyer, Gowanus Dredgers Canoe Club, Principles GI Coffee House, Back to John's Deli, Monte's, Strong Rope Brewery, Lavender Lake, Halyards, Pig Beach, Lowlands, Morbid Anatomy Museum, Voice of Gowanus, the Tide Mill Institute, Historic Districts Council, Lenape Center, and Sludgie the Whale.

Thank you to the generous Kickstarter backers who helped launch this book.

About the Author

Brad Vogel is author of the poetry collection *Broad Meadow Bird* (Euphrosine Publishing, 2015). A finalist for the 2020 Erksine J. Poetry Prize, his poetry appears in a variety of outlets. His writing has appeared in *The New York Times*. He founded and coordinates the **Gowanus Dawn Reading** (since 2017), a poetry reading in canoes on the Gowanus Canal; *NYC Poets Afloat* (since 2019), a residency and reading series aboard vessels around New York Harbor; and **Gowanustasia** (since 2023), a poetry series at Principles GI Coffee House. Brad coordinated the **Bridges of Brass** and **Boat for the Vote!** on-water Gowanus extravaganzas, and founded the annual **Pride Paddle on the Gowanus** (since 2018).

Brad served as captain of the **Gowanus Dredgers Canoe Club** from 2017-2022 and served on the **Gowanus Superfund Community Advisory Group** from 2017-2021. He co-founded the **Gowanus Landmarking Coalition** and was a member of **Voice of Gowanus**, performing in Café Rezoné during the pandemic. He showed work in **Gowanus Open Studios** (2019) and took part in the **Gowanus Night Heron** arts collective event in 2021 (pictured at right). He was honored by former Brooklyn Borough President Eric Adams for pandemic mutual aide response volunteer work. Brad previously practiced as an attorney, served as a non-profit executive, and works in sustainable shipping.

Reciting at Gowanus Night Heron, 2021

www.ingramcontent.com/pod-product-compliance
Lightning Source LLC
Chambersburg PA
CBHW051241120626
46547CB00014B/1750